MICHAEL JACKSON

THE WORLD SAYS GOODBYE TO THE KING OF POP

1958 - 2009

MICHAEL**JACKSON**

THE WORLD SAYS GOODBYE TO THE KING OF POP

1958 · 2009

Excluding certain works, whose copyright may or may not be noted, ©2009 Whitman Publishing, LLC
3101 Clairmont Road · Suite C · Atlanta GA 30329

This book was prepared for educational and informational purposes regarding the life of Michael Jackson. The publication includes material from a wide variety of sources, as well as commentary and analysis regarding such material. Whitman Publishing is not affiliated with or endorsed by any individuals, organizations or entities referenced in this book.

Correspondence concerning this book may be directed to the publisher, at the address above.

ISBN: 0794829287
Printed and assembled in United States of America

For a catalog of collectibles-related books, supplies and storage products, visit Whitman Publishing online at **www.whitmanbooks.com**.

This collection of photographs and condolences pays tribute to Michael Jackson, his career and his fans.

Michael's career started at age 10 in 1968 when he became the lead singer in his family's musical group, the Jackson 5. The Jacksons were regulars on television shows, their records soared up the charts and a fandom was beginning to swell around the world.

The solo career of Michael was even more impressive. He was an annual recipient of music awards, his concerts were sellouts and he blew everyone away with his trademark "Moonwalk." He met with U.S. presidents, discussed humanitarian missions with foreign dignitaries and influenced the future careers of youth across the globe.

In this tribute, the photos from the King of Pop's childhood will bring back memories, the concert images will move you just like his music does, and scenes of mourning fans will illustrate the love and adoration he enjoyed around the world.

This book is a celebration of Michael's life.

"I knew Michael as a child and watched him grow over the years. Of all the thousands of entertainers I have worked with, Michael was THE most outstanding. Many have tried and will try to copy him, but his talent will never be matched.**"**

— Dick Clark
former host of "American Bandstand"

AT 10 YEARS OLD, MICHAEL JACKSON BECAME THE LEAD SINGER IN HIS FAMILY'S MUSICAL GROUP, THE JACKSON 5, SHOWN HERE IN LOS ANGELES. WITH MICHAEL (FRONT RIGHT) ARE BROTHERS (FROM LEFT) TITO, 16; MARLON, 11; JACKIE, 19; AND JERMAINE, 14. (AP PHOTO).

" We have lost an icon in our industry. He will live on in my memory and most definitely through the music he shared with so many. **"**

— Dionne Warwick,
singer and Michael's friend

THIRTEEN-YEAR-OLD MICHAEL SINGS IN THE FAMILY'S ENCINO, CALIFORNIA, HOME IN 1972. (AP PHOTO).

"Rarely has the world received a gift with the magnitude of artistry, talent and vision as Michael Jackson. He was a true musical icon whose identifiable voice, innovative dance moves, stunning musical versatility and sheer star power carried him from childhood to worldwide acclaim."

— Neil Portnow,
president of The Recording Academy

BY AGE 13, MICHAEL WAS RECEIVING BAGS FULL OF CARDS AND LETTERS FROM FANS. (AP PHOTO).

"When I think of him, I think of this young boy, this teenager I first met. He was a great teenager, optimistic and adorable. A great singer...a genius like Ray Charles. He had a gift. He was able to connect with people."

— Cher

THE JACKSON 5, (FROM LEFT) TITO, MARLON, MICHAEL, JACKIE AND JERMAINE, PERFORM DURING THE "SONNY AND CHER COMEDY HOUR" IN LOS ANGELES ON SEPT. 15, 1972. (AP PHOTO).

"(As a boy) he always wanted to be the best, and he was willing to work as hard as it took to be that. And we could all see that he was a winner at that age. And I've always believed winners are winners long before they win. And picking them out before they win is very easy with a Michael Jackson."

— Berry Gordy Jr.,
founder of Motown Records

TITO, RANDY, JACKIE, MARLON AND MICHAEL PERFORM ON "THE TONIGHT SHOW STARRING JOHNNY CARSON" ON JUNE 21, 1976.

(PHOTO BY FRAKN CARROLL/NBCU PHOTO BANK VIA AP IMAGES).

" Michael Jackson showed me that you can actually see the beat. He made the music come to life! He made me believe in magic. I will miss him! "

— P Diddy,
musician

MICHAEL (CENTER) SHARES THE SPOTLIGHT ON THE JACKSONS' TELEVISION SHOW WITH (LEFT TO RIGHT) RANDY, LA TOYA, MARLON, JANET, JACKIE, MAUREEN AND TITO. (ISAAC SUTTON/EBONY COLLECTION VIA AP IMAGES).

❝I feel privileged to have hung out and worked with Michael. He was a massively talented boy-man with a gentle soul. His music will be remembered forever and my memories of our time together will be happy ones.**❞**

— Paul McCartney,
musician

MICHAEL WITH LOLLA FALONA DURING THE 1977 AMERICAN MUSIC AWARDS. (AP PHOTO).

"I can't stop crying; this is too sudden and shocking. I am unable to imagine this. My heart is hurting. I am in prayer for his kids and the family.**"**

— Diana Ross,
entertainer, Michael's friend and co-star in "The Wiz"

MICHAEL POSES WITH CO-STARS DIANA ROSS AND NIPSY RUSSELL AT A NEWS CONFERENCE FOR "THE WIZ" IN NEW YORK CITY ON SEPT. 28, 1977. (AP PHOTO/SUZANNE VLAMIS).

" Just as there will never be another Fred Astaire or Chuck Berry or Elvis Presley, there will never be anyone comparable to Michael Jackson. His talent, his wonderment and his mystery make him legend. **"**

— Stephen Spielberg,
director

MICHAEL (RIGHT) AS THE SCARECROW, DIANA ROSS (CENTER) AS DOROTHY AND NIPSEY RUSSELL AS THE TINMAN DURING FILMING OF THE MUSICAL "THE WIZ" IN NEW YORK'S WORLD TRADE CENTER ON TUESDAY, OCT. 4, 1977. TED ROSS, PORTRAYING THE LION, IS PARTLY HIDDEN BEHIND RUSSELL. THE MUSICAL WAS BASED ON "THE WIZARD OF OZ." (AP PHOTO).

" The world has lost an icon and music has lost treasures. He wrote songs that generations of yesterday, today and tomorrow will all keep on singing. **"**

— Sophia Loren,
actress

MICHAEL LAUGHS WITH HIS SISTERS JANET AND LA TOYA IN 1979. (ISAAC SUTTON/EBONY COLLECTION VIA AP IMAGES).

" He was the consummate entertainer and his contributions and legacy will be felt upon the world forever. I've lost my little brother today, and part of my soul has gone with him. **"**

— Quincy Jones,
record producer

MARLON AND MICHAEL WITH SUPERSTAR PRODUCER QUINCY JONES AT HOLLYWOOD'S BROWN DERBY IN 1980.

(ISAAC SUTTON/EBONY COLLECTION VIA AP IMAGES).

"I can't speak highly enough about what I got to witness every single night for nearly two years, which was the brilliance of someone who was truly innovative. Before 1984, no one had ever seen moves like that...You can see how deeply effective he was as an R&B artist.**"**

— Sheryl Crow,
musician and former backup singer for Michael

MICHAEL AND DIANA ROSS HOLD THEIR AMERICAN MUSIC AWARDS IN LOS ANGELES ON JAN. 30, 1981. JACKSON WON FOR FAVORITE SOUL ALBUM AND ROSS WON FOR FAVORITE FEMALE SOUL VOCALIST. (AP PHOTO).

"Michael Jackson was extraordinary. When we worked together on "Bad," I was in awe of his absolute mastery of movement on the one hand, and of the music on the other. Every step he took was absolutely precise and fluid at the same time. It was like watching quicksilver in motion. He was wonderful to work with, an absolute professional at all times, and — it really goes without saying — a true artist."

— Martin Scorsese,
director

MICHAEL AND HIS FIVE BROTHERS ON THE SET OF A PEPSI-COLA COMMERCIAL IN 1984. FROM LEFT TO RIGHT ARE TITO, JERMAINE, JACKIE, MICHAEL, RANDY AND MARLON. (AP PHOTO).

"I had the pleasure of working with Michael on 'Beat It' back in '83 — one of my fondest memories in my career. Michael will be missed and may he rest in peace.**"**

— Eddie Van Halen,
musician

GUITARIST EDDIE VAN HALEN MAKES A GUEST APPEARANCE DURING MICHAEL'S VICTORY TOUR CONCERT IN IRVING, TEXAS, IN 1984. VAN HALEN JOINS IN DURING MICHAEL'S HIT "BEAT IT." (AP PHOTO/CARLOS OSORIO).

"The incomparable Michael Jackson has made a bigger impact on music than any other artist in the history of music. He was magic. He was what we all strive to be. He will always be the King of Pop! Life is not about how many breaths you take, but about how many moments in life that take your breath away. For anyone who has ever seen, felt or heard his art, we are all honored to have been alive in this generation to experience the magic of Michael Jackson. I love you, Michael."

— Beyonce Knowles,
entertainer

MICHAEL IS JOINED BY HIS SISTERS (LEFT TO RIGHT) MAUREEN "REBIE," JANET AND LA TOYA ON STAGE DURING THE 26TH ANNUAL GRAMMY AWARDS IN LOS ANGELES IN 1984, AS MICHAEL RECEIVES AN AWARD FOR MALE POP VOCAL. (AP PHOTO/DOUG PIZAC).

66 My heart is overcome with sadness for the devastating loss of my true friend Michael. He was an extraordinary friend, artist and contributor to the world. I join his family and his fans in celebrating his incredible life and mourning his untimely passing. **99**

— Brooke Shields,
actress and close friend of Michael

MICHAEL ESCORTS ACTRESS-MODEL BROOKE SHIELDS TO A PARTY AT THE REX RESTAURANT IN LOS ANGELES FOLLOWING THE GRAMMY AWARDS PRESENTATION IN 1984. (AP PHOTO/RUSSELL TURIAK).

" Michael was a pop phenomenon who never stopped pushing the envelope of creativity. Michael was undoubtedly a great entertainer and his popularity spanned generations and the globe. **"**

— Arnold Schwarzenegger

MICHAEL WALKS WITH PRESIDENT RONALD REAGAN ON THE SOUTH LAWN OF THE WHITE HOUSE ON MONDAY, MAY 14, 1984, WHERE REAGAN PRESENTED MICHAEL AN AWARD FOR HIS PART IN A NATIONAL CAMPAIGN AGAINST DRUNK DRIVING. (AP PHOTO/SCOTT STEWART).

" Michael's example of musical artistry was rooted in the proud tradition of black American music. His career trajectory — from the working-class streets of industrial Gary, Indiana, during the post World War II boom, to the heights of the entertainment industry — is a classic example of black American achievement, and of the American Dream. **"**

— Benjamin Todd Jealous,
NAACP president.

MICHAEL RECEIVES THE HOLLYWOOD WALK OF FAME AWARD FROM LOS ANGELES MAYOR TOM BRADLEY AND HONORARY MAYOR JOHNNY GRANT ON NOV. 20, 1984. (ROBERT JOHNSON/EBONY COLLECTION VIA AP IMAGES).

" Let us remember him for his unparalleled contribution to the world of music, his generosity of spirit in his quest to heal the world and the joy he brought to his millions of devoted fans throughout the world. I feel blessed to have performed with him several times and to call him my friend. No artist will ever take his place. His star will shine forever. "

— Mariah Carey,
entertainer

MICHAEL ONSTAGE ON OPENING NIGHT OF HIS VICTORY TOUR AT DODGER STADIUM IN LOS ANGELES ON DEC. 1, 1984.
(AP PHOTO/LENNOX MCLENDON).

ff He broke barriers, he changed radio formats. With music, he made it possible for people like Oprah Winfrey and Barack Obama to impact the mainstream world. His legacy is unparalleled. ™™

— Usher,
musician

GRAMMY WINNERS DIONNE WARWICK, STEVIE WONDER, QUINCY JONES, MICHAEL JACKSON AND LIONEL RICHIE POSE TOGETHER
BACKSTAGE AT THE GRAMMY AWARDS SHOW IN LOS ANGELES ON FEB. 26, 1986. (AP PHOTO).

"Rest in peace Mike…You were 100 percent original. We will always love, miss and remember your greatness."

— Ice-T,
musician, actor

MICHAEL OPENS THE FIRST OF THREE CONCERTS PROMOTING HIS "BAD" ALBUM IN ROSEMONT, ILLINOIS, ON APRIL 19, 1988.
(AP PHOTO/MARK ELIAS).

"I knew Michael since the mid-70s, but we got tight in the '80s because by then James Brown had kind of adopted me as a son, and Michael was a James Brown fanatic. He used to always come to see James Brown…I hope now the genius and humanity of Michael Jackson gets its due."

— Reverend Al Sharpton

MICHAEL STRUTS WITH STYLE DURING A 1988 CONCERT. (PHOTO BY KEVIN MAZUR/WIREIMAGE).

"I have to say to you that Michael Jackson's been an idol for me all my life. I remember being in my house when I was very, very young and having his posters above my bed."

— Celine Dion,
entertainer

MICHAEL'S "BAD" TOUR DREW 4.4 MILLION PEOPLE OVER 123 DATES. (PHOTO BY KEVIN MAZUR/WIREIMAGE).

" Michael Jackson was a brilliant troubadour for his generation, a genius whose music reflected the passion and creativity of an era. His artistry and magnetism changed the music landscape forever. We have been profoundly affected by his originality, creativity and amazing body of work. **"**

— Howard Stringer,
chairman, CEO and president, Sony Corporation

IN 1990, MICHAEL'S "LEAVE ME ALONE" WON A GRAMMY FOR BEST MUSIC VIDEO, SHORT FORM. (PHOTO BY KEVIN MAZUR/WIREIMAGE).

"He was idolized by many New Yorkers both young and old....I think it's fair to say he really was a one-of-a-kind music talent and I just want his family and loved ones to know that New Yorkers are thinking of them and that the king of pop will always be remembered here in the entertainment capital of the world, and I will always be listening to his music. **"**

— Michael Bloomberg, mayor of New York City

MICHAEL IN NEW YORK CITY IN 1992. (AP PHOTO/RICHARD DREW).

" I was lucky enough to know and work with Michael Jackson in his prime. Michael was an extraordinary talent and a truly great international star. **"**

— John Landis,
director of "Thriller"

MICHAEL PERFORMS DURING THE HALFTIME SHOW AT SUPER BOWL XXVII IN PASADENA, CALIFORNIA, JAN. 31, 1993.
(AP PHOTO/RUSTY KENNEDY).

"I loved Michael with all my soul and I can't imagine life without him. We had so much in common and we had such loving fun together. I was packing up my clothes to go to London for his opening when I heard the news. **"**

— Elizabeth Taylor,
actress

MICHAEL HOLDS HIS AWARD WHILE POSING WITH ACTRESS ELIZABETH TAYLOR AT THE 20TH AMERICAN MUSIC AWARDS AT THE SHRINE AUDITORIUM IN LOS ANGELES ON JAN. 25, 1993. (AP PHOTO/MARK TERRILL).

"I am so very sad and confused with every emotion possible. I am heartbroken for his children who I know were everything to him and for his family. This is such a massive loss on so many levels, words fail me. **"**

— Lisa Marie Presley,
Michael's former wife and daughter of Elvis Presley

MICHAEL AND LISA MARIE PRESLEY-JACKSON ACKNOWLEDGE APPLAUSE FROM THE AUDIENCE AFTER COMING OUT ONSTAGE
TO OPEN THE 11TH ANNUAL MTV VIDEO MUSIC AWARDS AT NEW YORK'S RADIO CITY MUSIC HALL ON SEPT. 8, 1994.
(AP PHOTO/BEBETO MATTHEWS).

"I met Michael Jackson at the age of 8 when his father and my new friend, Joe Jackson, first began to bring the Jackson 5 to Chicago from their home in Gary, Indiana, for concert appearances... Michael Jackson's personal crescendo of amazing power as an entertainer was clear and unmistakable and has never slowed to this very day! His passing will be grieved far beyond that of any other singer, composer, producer, dancer and choreographer in the history of the world. Indeed, in my very firmest personal belief, there will never, ever be another Michael Jackson. **"**

— Don Cornelius,
creator of TV show "Soul Train"

MICHAEL PERFORMS DURING THE 1995 MTV VIDEO MUSIC AWARDS AT RADIO CITY MUSIC HALL IN NEW YORK ON SEPT. 7, 1995.
(AP PHOTO/BEBETO MATTHEWS).

"He was a beautiful human being. If not for him, I wouldn't be doing what I'm doing. He gave me joy as a child and showed me the way to go.**"**

— Lenny Kravitz,
musician

IN 1995, MICHAEL RELEASED THE DOUBLE ALBUM "HISTORY: PAST, PRESENT AND FUTURE, BOOK I," WHICH INCLUDED HIS GREATEST HITS AND NEW SONGS. (PHOTO BY KEVIN MAZUR/WIREIMAGE).

" The Nelson Mandela Foundation regrets the untimely passing of Michael Jackson. His loss will be felt by his fans world-wide. **"**

— Achmat Dangor,
chief executive officer of the Nelson Mandela Foundation

MICHAEL JACKSON HUGS FORMER SOUTH AFRICAN PRESIDENT NELSON MANDELA IN PRETORIA, SOUTH AFRICA, ON JULY 20, 1996.

66 I feel like his music will never die and his spirit will never die, because he influenced so many if us. He gave us a lot of hope that we feel like we can be big. He was very inspiring and up close and personal with his fans. That to me was special. That's one of the things that I loved about Mike. When I got a chance to meet him, that's the feeling and spirit that I got from him. **99**

— Snoop Dogg,
entertainer

MICHAEL PERFORMS DURING A CONCERT IN AMSTERDAM ON SEPT. 28, 1996, AS A PART OF HIS "HISTORY" WORLD TOUR.
(AP PHOTO/DUSAN VRANIC).

" Michael Jackson was my musical God. He made me believe that all things are possible, and through real and positive music. He can live forever! I love Michael Jackson. God Bless him. "

— Wyclef Jean,
musician

MICHAEL WITH MODEL/ACTRESS BROOKE SHIELDS, BROTHER JACKIE, MOTHER KATHERINE AND FATHER JOE.
(ISAAC SUTTON/EBONY COLLECTION VIA AP IMAGES).

"We have lost a genius and a true ambassador of not only pop music, but of all music. He has been an inspiration to multiple generations and I will always cherish the moments I shared with him on stage and all of the things I learned about music from him and the time we spent together.**"**

— Justin Timberlake,
musician

MICHAEL POINTS TO FANS DURING A PRESS CONFERENCE AT MUNICH'S OLYMPIC STADIUM ON JUNE 9, 1999. HE VISITED TO PROMOTE HIS JUNE 27 CHARITY CONCERT "MICHAEL JACKSON AND FRIENDS." (AP PHOTO/UWE LEIN).

" I salute you King of Pop. You made the whole world moonwalk together. **"**

— LL Cool J,
entertainer

MICHAEL PERFORMS WITH GUITARIST SLASH DURING THE BENEFIT CONCERT "MICHAEL JACKSON & FRIENDS" AT THE MUNICH OLYMPIC STADIUM, JUNE 27 1999. THE PROCEEDS OF THE SHOW WENT TO THE RED CROSS, THE UNITED NATIONS EDUCATIONAL SCIENTIFIC AND CULTURAL ORGANIZATION, AND THE NELSON MANDELA CHILDREN'S FUND. (AP PHOTO/UWE LEIN).

" I think we'll mourn his loss as well as the loss of ourselves as children listening to 'Thriller' on the record player. A major strand of our cultural DNA has left us. **"**

— John Mayer,
musician

MICHAEL HOLDS THE MILLENNIUM AWARD THAT WAS AWARDED TO HIM AT THE 2000 WORLD MUSIC AWARDS IN MONACO, FRENCH RIVIERA, MAY 10, 2000. (AP PHOTO/LIONEL CIRONNEAU).

66 As a child of the '80s, I feel as though his music and his videos have been an inseparable part of my life and that of an entire generation. And the powerful thing about great music is that it will always live on. He was and always will be an icon. 99

— John Legend,
entertainer

MICHAEL GESTURES AFTER BEING INDUCTED INTO THE ROCK AND ROLL HALL OF FAME ON MONDAY, MARCH 19, 2001.

(AP PHOTO/KATHY WILLENS).

" Michael Jackson was my generation's most iconic cultural hero. Courageous, unique and incredibly talented. He'll be missed greatly. **"**

— Russell Simmons,
founder of Def-Jam records

MICHAEL SPORTS HIS TRADEMARK GLOVE AS HE PERFORMS "BILLIE JEAN" DURING HIS "30TH ANNIVERSARY CELEBRATION, THE SOLO YEARS" CONCERT AT NEW YORK'S MADISON SQUARE GARDEN, SEPT. 7, 2001. (AP PHOTO/BETH A. KEISER).

"I am truly saddened that my mentor, brother and friend will no longer be with us physically. At the same time I feel so blessed to have been touched by his music, his dance, his lyrics and his pure genius. It is because of Michael's yesterday that I am who I am today! Michael Jackson rest in peace and may your music and legacy forever reign on Earth!**"**

— R. Kelly,
musician

MICHAEL ACCEPTS HIS AWARD AS ARTIST OF THE CENTURY AT THE 29TH AMERICAN MUSIC AWARDS IN LOS ANGELES, JAN. 9, 2002.

(AP PHOTO/KEVORK DJANSEZIAN).

66 He is a musical icon. I have always said tomyself that the top would be working with Michael and last year when I got the chance to work with him, I was completely humbled....Michael Jackson's accomplished so much that there's not even words to explain what he's done for urban and pop music. Everyartist that I personally know has been influenced by him. The world has lost one of the greatest entertainers who shaped many generations and will continue to for years to come. 99

— Akon,
musician

MICHAEL PERFORMS AT A DEMOCRATIC NATIONAL COMMITTEE FUNDRAISER AT THE APOLLO THEATRE IN NEW YORK, APRIL 24, 2002.
(AP PHOTO/MARK LENNIHAN).

(AP Photo/Joel Ryan)

Michael's Last Appearance...

Michael Jackson's last public appearance was at the London O2 Arena on Thursday, March 5, 2009, to announce he was set to play 10 live concerts at the arena in July 2009.

(AP Photo/Joel Ryan)

The King of Pop Passes Away...

People gather outside a window with a Michael Jackson statue in it at Madame Tussauds in New York, Friday, June 26, 2009, a day after the passing of The King of Pop in Los Angeles.

LEILA MCGUIRE OF ANAHEIM, CALIFORNIA, LAYS DOWN A FLOWER ON MICHAEL'S STAR ON THE HOLLYWOOD WALK OF FAME IN LOS ANGELES EARLY FRIDAY MORNING, JUNE 26, 2009. (AP PHOTO/CHRIS PIZZELLO).

" Michael Jackson was a spectacular performer, a music icon. Everyone remembers hearing his songs, watching him moonwalk on television during Motown's 25th anniversary…His condolences went out to the Jackson family and fans who [are mourning] his loss. **"**

— White House press secretary Robert Gibbs conveying President Obama's reaction to the loss of Michael

A LARGE CROWD GATHERS OUTSIDE THE APOLLO THEATER IN THE HARLEM SECTION OF NEW YORK TO PAY TRIBUTE TO MICHAEL ON JUNE 25, 2009. (AP PHOTO/LOUIS LANZANO).

"Death comes to all. But great achievements build a monument. He IS and WAS the greatest entertainer of all times...Peace to you brother.**"**

— Star Jones,
television personality

OROCK OROCK HOLDS A SIGN OUTSIDE THE UCLA MEDICAL CENTER IN LOS ANGELES, WHERE MICHAEL WAS TAKEN JUNE 25, 2009.

HE WAS 50 YEARS OLD AT THE TIME OF HIS DEATH. (AP PHOTO/MATT SAYLES).

"Michael Jackson was my inspiration."

— Miley Cyrus,
entertainer

PEOPLE IN NEW YORK'S TIMES SQUARE REACT TO THE NEWS THAT MICHAEL DIED THURSDAY, JUNE 25, 2009. (AP PHOTO/MARY ALTAFFER).

" I come to you today with great sadness, acknowledging the loss of the greatest entertainer in the history of mankind. For me he was more than that, he was my idol, he was a role model, he was someone to cry to when my childhood was unbearable, he was a brother, he was a dear friend. "

— Corey Feldman,
actor

FIVE-YEAR-OLD NEHEMIAH WILLIAMS (SECOND FROM LEFT) LOOKS AT THE FLOWERS AND TEDDY BEARS LEFT ON THE FRONT PORCH OF MICHAEL'S CHILDHOOD HOME IN GARY, INDIANA. (AP PHOTO/JOHN SMIERCIAK).

" It's a very sad day for the pop industry, especially for us, as we looked up to him and his work. **"**

— Black Eyed Peas

A MOTORCYCLE COURIER READS AN AFTERNOON PAPER IN KUALA LUMPUR, MALAYSIA, WITH THE ANNOUNCEMENT THAT MICHAEL HAD DIED. (AP PHOTO/MARK BAKER).

" Michael…Never Can Say Goodbye, I Want You Back, You're Out Of My Life, It's So Hard To Say Goodbye, I am going to miss you M.J. Thank you for your music that uplifted many of us. We luv you and we will miss you always. "

— Christina Johnson Reed,
Austin, Texas

FANS HOLD UP A SEA OF SINGLE-GLOVED HANDS IN AN IMPROMPTU CELEBRATION OF THE LIFE OF MICHAEL OUTSIDE UCLA MEDICAL CENTER IN LOS ANGELES AFTER HE WAS PRONOUNCED DEAD. (AP PHOTO/REED SAXON).

66 Michael, thank you so much for sharing your gift of music with the world! I will never forget the first time I heard you sing when I was a child. I knew right then, I was a fan for life!!! 99

— Kiera Griffith,
Cartersville, Georgia

A FILIPINO CUSTOMER WATCHES MICHAEL'S "THRILLER" VIDEO CLIP AS HE SHOPS FOR A TELEVISION SET AT A USED TV SHOP IN MANILA, PHILIPPINES, ON FRIDAY JUNE 26, 2009. (AP PHOTO/BULLIT MARQUEZ).

" Michael, you were truly the King of Pop. You touch so many lives with your music and you caring heart. You are and will always be an inspiration to the music industry. We can never say goodbye. "

— Shondrae DeRouen,
Darrow, Louisiana

追悼
MICHAEL JACKSON
＜KING OF POP＞マイケル・ジャクソンが現地時間の25日、
心肺停止状態でUCLA病院に搬送され、
同日午後2時26分に死去。享年50歳。
謹んでご冥福をお祈りいたします。

PEOPLE WATCH A MICHAEL JACKSON DVD IN FRONT OF A SPECIAL SECTION IN MEMORY OF THE LATE SUPERSTAR, SHOWCASING HIS CDS, DVDS AND VIDEOS, AT A TOWER RECORDS JAPAN STORE IN TOKYO, JAPAN, JUNE 26, 2009. JAPANESE FANS WERE ALWAYS AMONG MICHAEL'S MOST PASSIONATE SUPPORTERS. (AP PHOTO/KOJI SASAHARA).

66 Michael…You are an angel that gave the world love, devotion, music, dance and hope. I thank you for devoting your earthly life to giving so many unfortunate people food, clothes, medical care and a chance for continuance of life. The earth lost a great man on June 25, 2009, but heaven gained your beautiful spirit. 99

— Andrea Chandler,
Philadelphia, Pennsylvania

ONE BIG SCREEN SHOWS THE NEWS OF MICHAEL'S DEATH AT A SHOPPING DISTRICT IN HONG KONG. (AP PHOTO/KIN CHEUNG).

"MJ revolutionized every aspect of dance, music videos, MTV, live concerts and last the Grammys. The loss is irreplaceable.**"**

— Narendra Purabia,
Mumbai, India

A YOUNG RUSSIAN WOMAN FIXES A TRIBUTE TO MICHAEL TO THE FENCE SURROUNDING THE U.S. EMBASSY IN MOSCOW, RUSSIA.
(AP PHOTO/MIKHAIL METZEL).

" I'm sure you're singing and dancing and smiling in heaven. The legacy you created for generations will make sure that we will all be doing the same. You are a legend, a hero and an ambassador for all people young and old, black and white, male and female throughout the world. You will never be forgotten. Rest in peace dear Michael. **"**

— Ciro Ragozzino,
Sydney, New South Wales

CURATOR CURTIS HUBER PUTS A BLACK WREATH IN FRONT OF A WAX FIGURE OF MICHAEL AT THE WAX MUSEUM AT FISHERMAN'S WHARF IN SAN FRANCISCO. (AP PHOTO/JEFF CHIU).

" Michael, you and your music brought so much joy to my life. You will be so greatly missed. My prayers go out to your children and family. Thank you for all the memories your music has given to me and I will make sure your music lives on through my children one day. You were a remarkable person who will never be forgotten. You are irreplaceable, and you and your music will live on forever in our hearts. We love you Michael. God bless…Rest in peace. "

— Isabel Gonzales,
Cibolo, Texas

LORI WOLF LEAVES FLOWERS AT A MAKESHIFT MEMORIAL AT THE GATES OF MICHAEL'S FORMER RESIDENCE, NEVERLAND RANCH, TO PAY RESPECTS TO THE POP ICON. WOLF USED TO BRING HER KIDS TO THE RANCH WHEN MICHAEL WOULD OPEN UP THE AMUSEMENT PARK TO LOCAL CHILDREN. (AP PHOTO/MICHAEL A. MARIANT).

"You have done more than any President could do in life. You have taken the nations. I will miss you dearly MJ."

— Sharon Pinkston,
Hyattsville, Maryland

MOURNERS GATHER OUTSIDE THE GATES OF THE JACKSON FAMILY HOME IN ENCINO, CALIFORNIA. (AP PHOTO/KATY WINN).

" R.I.P. Michael! I know you will be Moonwalking around heaven. Bless the Jackson family. My heart goes out to you all! "

— Emma Bryant,
Detroit, Michigan

PEOPLE GATHER NEAR A MEMORIAL FOR MICHAEL ON THE FRONT LAWN OF HITSVILLE U.S.A., THE MOTOWN MUSEUM IN DETROIT, MICHIGAN, SATURDAY, JUNE 27, 2009, FOR A THIRD DAY OF REMEMBRANCE. (AP PHOTO/THE DETROIT NEWS/JOHN T. GREILICK).

" Everybody's talking about his passing but I'm talking about his living. His great brilliance; so much brilliance that in 50 years they'll still be discovering brilliance that he produced. I guess they'll compare him with Bob Marley and Elvis but so many of these young peopledon't really know who Michael was. They dance to his music but they don't know the spark behind him. "

— Al Peterson,
Westchester County, New York

A CROWD GATHERS OUTSIDE LIVERPOOL STREET STATION IN LONDON TO PAY TRIBUTE TO MICHAEL. (IAN WEST/PA WIRE/AP IMAGES).

"I feel like part of my heart is gone. I was in love with him ever since I was little. I did the moonwalk, I did it all.**"**

— Patty Lee,
Dallas, Texas

FANS LOOK AT A SHRINE TO MICHAEL OUTSIDE A STORE IN LEICESTER SQUARE, LONDON, ENGLAND, JUNE 28, 2009.

(OWEN HUMPHREYS/PA WIRE/AP IMAGES).

"He was a kind, genuine and wonderful man. He was also one of the greatest entertainers that ever lived. I loved him very much and I will miss him every remaining day of my life.**"**

— Liza Minnelli,
entertainer and friend of Michael's

FANS OF MICHAEL STAND NEXT TO POSTERS DURING A VIGIL OUTSIDE THE SFORZESCO CASTLE IN MILAN, ITALY, ON SATURDAY, JUNE 27, 2009. (AP PHOTO/LUCA BRUNO).

" I think the word you've got to use is 'electrifying.' It was absolutely electrifying. He wasn't just singing about 'Thriller' — he actually was a thriller in every sense of that term. I think it's the voice in conjunction with that incredible sense of rhythm and timing and innovation that made him the icon that he will always be. **"**

— Jason King,
music professor at New York University

YOUNG FANS HOLD A POSTER OF MICHAEL AT THE APOLLO THEATER IN THE HARLEM NEIGHBORHOOD OF NEW YORK. "I LOVE MICHAEL JACKSON. HE IS MY INSPIRATION," SAID NINA KOLLBRUNNE (LEFT) FROM SWEDEN. (AP PHOTO/YANINA MANOLOVA).

" In one of the darkest moments of our lives we find it hard to find the words appropriate to this sudden tragedy we all had to encounter. Our beloved son, brother and father of three children has gone so unexpectedly, in such a tragic way and much too soon…We want to thank all of his faithful supporters and loyal fans worldwide, you who Michael loved so much. Please do not despair, because Michael will continue to live on in each and every one of you. Continue to spread his message, because that is what he would want you to do. Carry on, so his legacy will live forever. **"**

— The Jackson Family,
June 28, 2009

A GROUP OF FANS STAND AMONGST FLOWERS AT A SHRINE TO MICHAEL OUTSIDE THE O2 ARENA IN LONDON, JUNE 27, 2009.

(JOHN STILLWELL/PA WIRE/AP IMAGES).

"My heart is heavy because my idol died."

— Byron Garcia,
security consultant at a Philippine prison who organized
the famous video of 1,500 inmates doing a synchronized
dance to "Thriller."

FILIPINO INMATES PERFORM A "THRILLER" TRIBUTE TO MICHAEL INSIDE THE CEBU PROVINCIAL DETENTION AND REHABILITATION CENTER IN THE CENTRAL PHILIPPINES ON SATURDAY, JUNE 27, 2009. (AP PHOTO).